THE REMINISCENCES OF
Mr. Paul D. Richmond

INTERVIEWED BY
Paul Stillwell

U.S. Naval Institute • Annapolis, Maryland

Copyright © 2014

Preface

This oral history was the result of a series of interviews I began in October 1986 to record the memories of the eight surviving members of the Golden Thirteen. They were the Navy's first black officers, commissioned in 1944. During the course of those interviews, I learned that the individual who devised the curriculum for the training period during World War II had been a Naval Reserve officer, Paul D. Richmond, who was a Naval Academy graduate. The Naval Academy alumni register provided his address, and in 1990 I went to the Detroit area to interview him. Richmond and his wife Virginia were gracious hosts, and the interview was a valuable one. Richmond's perspective—as a result of working with the group, but not being part of it—was most useful. Some of the members of the group thought that the training period was an experiment on the part of the Navy and that the service had set them up to fail. In this interview Mr. Richmond explained that it was no experiment. His assignment was to make the men officers and that he made the course difficult so that they would be as well trained as they could be. In 1993 the Naval Institute Press published the book *The Golden Thirteen: Recollections of the First Black Naval Officers*. One of the chapters was drawn from the following interview with Richmond. He and I both did some editing of the raw transcript to arrive at the completed version. This transcript contains additional material that was not in the book.

Thanks go to Ms. Janis Jorgensen of the Naval Institute staff who has coordinated the printing and binding of the finished product. In completing this volume, the Naval Institute expresses its gratitude to the Tawani Foundation and the Pritzker Military Library of Chicago for their generous financial support of the oral history program that produced this memoir.

Paul Stillwell
U.S. Naval Institute
August 2014

PAUL DEMING RICHMOND

Paul D. Richmond was born in Detroit, Michigan, on 7 November 1920. When he was ten years old, his father died. The son went to Connecticut to spend the summer with an uncle and his family, which included a son about Paul's age. One family outing was to New London to visit the USS *Constitution*, the War of 1812 ship nicknamed "Old Ironsides." Both boys were so dazzled by it that they vowed to become naval officers.

Some years later, when Richmond was in a senior high school civics class, the instructor proposed a term project in which each student was to submit the name of a government position in which he might be interested. Richmond's interest in becoming a naval officer apparently piqued the instructor's attention, and he decided to use it as the class project and explore the possibilities. Richmond was able to secure an appointment to the Naval Academy and a seat in preparatory school.

In his senior year, Richmond went on a class trip to Washington and met his Michigan congressman in his office on Capitol Hill. The congressman was so generous as to lend his car to Richmond and a friend so they could go to Annapolis and visit his future college, which he later entered in the summer of 1938 as a plebe. Suitably impressed, Richmond voted for the congressman in later elections, even though the young man came from a staunchly Republican family.

The graduation for the class of 1942, of which Richmond was a member, took place on 19 December 1941 because the curriculum had previously been cut short with war on the horizon. Indeed, the Japanese struck Pearl Harbor two weeks before the class graduated. Because Richmond was an "eye unsat"—not able to meet the Navy's rigid vision standards—he was commissioned as a Naval Reserve officer, rather than regular Navy, and sent to shore duty instead of the fleet.

His first assignment was to the Great Lakes Naval Training Station north of Chicago. There he was part of the staff for boot camp, that is, training of recruits who had just joined the Navy and were on their way to active wartime service. Subsequently, he was reassigned to Camp Robert Smalls, a division of the training station that dealt exclusively with Negro sailors at a time when the various camps were segregated by race. In early 1944, using his Naval Academy experience as a basis, Richmond devised the curriculum and helped train the first contingent of black Naval Reserve officers. This group, which comprised 12 ensigns and one warrant officer, later became known as the Golden Thirteen.

After his service at Great Lakes, Richmond got into combat duty when he joined the staff of Rear Admiral John L. Hall, who was part of the Pacific Fleet Amphibious Force. Hall commanded the Southern Attack Force (Task Force 55) during the U.S. invasion of the island of Okinawa in the spring of 1945. Richmond later served with Hall in Hawaii and still later was an assistant port director in Tokyo Bay after the Allied capture of Japan.

Following war's end, Richmond returned to civilian life and resigned his commission because he believed that his reserve status and vision problem would prevent him from competing for career advancement with his counterparts in the regular Navy. Back in the United States, Richmond met a Detroit man who was embarking on a training program with Merrill-Lynch. Richmond was selected for the program and took part in a six-month training course in New York. He then joined the firm's Detroit office and thus began a 43-year career in the brokerage business.

Prior to his death on 14 June 2006, Richmond enjoyed 56 years of marriage with his wife, the former Virginia Chope. They traveled extensively, circling the globe on one of their many trips. He was a member of the Detroit Athletic Club and Rotary International.

Authorization

The U. S. Naval Institute is hereby authorized to make available to individuals, libraries, and other repositories of its choosing the transcripts of one oral history interview concerning the naval service of the undersigned. The interview was recorded on 14 January 1990 in collaboration with Paul Stillwell for the U.S. Naval Institute.

The undersigned does hereby release and assign to the U.S. Naval Institute all right, title, restrictions, and interest in the interview. The copyright in both the oral and transcribed version shall be the sole property of the U.S. Naval Institute. The tape recordings of the interviews are and will remain the property of the U.S. Naval Institute.

Signed and sealed this 27th day of January 1990.

Paul D. Richmond

Interview with Mr. Paul D. Richmond
Place: Mr. Richmond's home, Birmingham, Michigan
Date: Sunday, 14 January 1990

Paul Stillwell: Mr. Richmond, just for a little background, could you describe briefly your boyhood and what sort of a racial atmosphere you were raised in?

Mr. Richmond: Well, Paul, I grew up for the most part here in Detroit, Michigan. I was born in Detroit. I did live for a while down in Illinois, where my father ran a water-power company. But he died in 1931, when I was ten years old, and so my mother moved our family back to Detroit at that time, because she was a native Detroiter. And so, from that time on, I grew up in Highland Park, Michigan.[*] There were quite a number of blacks around the city at that time, and I was very familiar with them. I had no prejudice against them whatsoever. When I graduated from high school in 1938, I had been given a principal appointment to the Naval Academy.[†] Incidentally, it had been a long wish of mine to go to the academy, and I was just delighted to get this appointment. I passed the entrance exam, the physical exam, and entered the academy in the summer of '38 as part of the class of 1942.

So I went through the training. Because the war was developing, Congress in 1940 passed the universal conscription act, and the Army began drafting college men. At the same time, the academy programs were accelerated so that we had a date set for us at that time to graduate on December 19, 1941. As things developed, Pearl Harbor occurred on December 7, and then we graduated on the 19th. I had asked to be assigned to the battleship *Nevada*, but, as you know, it was damaged at Pearl Harbor, and a number of

---

[*] Highland Park is a city within the larger city of Detroit. Highland Park was the site of the Ford Motor Company offices and the factory where the famous Ford Model T was built over a period of 15 to 20 years before the whole complex was moved in 1928 to Dearborn, Michigan.
[†] The most desirable opportunity was a congressman's principal appointment for a particular opening at the Naval Academy. Someone with an alternate appointment would get in only if the person with the principal appointment was found to be unqualified or if he decided not to accept the appointment.

the other ships were completely out of commission.* Our class was reassigned to various places, and I was reassigned to the Great Lakes training station.†

Paul Stillwell: Why there in particular—do you know?

Mr. Richmond: No, I don't really know. I forgot to mention that while I was at the Naval Academy my eyesight deteriorated, and I was not given a commission in the regular Navy. I received a commission in the reserves along with maybe 20 or so other midshipmen with the same trouble. It's not unusual for young men of that age to develop myopia. So I was sent to the training station with the idea that I wasn't eligible for sea duty right away.

Paul Stillwell: Had you gone to integrated schools when you were growing up?

Mr. Richmond: Absolutely. There were numerous ethnic groups in Highland Park: Swedes, Polish, Italians, Armenians, and a few blacks—but not many.

Paul Stillwell: What sorts of assignments did you get into then at Great Lakes?

Mr. Richmond: I reported in on January 2. The main thing was the training of recruits that were coming in. The station was quite small in January of '42. There were very few academy men there. There was the admiral, who was the commandant of the Ninth Naval District.‡ There was the captain of the base.§ They were both Naval Academy men. There was an officer, Harold Edgar, who was in charge of recruit training; he was

---

* USS *Nevada* (BB-36) was the only battleship to get under way during the Japanese attack at Pearl Harbor on 7 December 1941. She was hit by bombs and then beached to avoid being sunk in the entrance channel to the harbor. The ship did not return to active service until early 1943 and thus had little need for a full crew in the meantime.
† Great Lakes, Illinois, a town on the shore of Lake Michigan, about 30 miles north of downtown Chicago, was the site of a large naval training station that included recruit training and a number of specialized schools. It is now known as Great Lakes Naval Training Center.
‡ Rear Admiral John Downes, USN, was Commandant Ninth Naval District and commanding officer of the Great Lakes Naval Training Station from August 1940 to January 1944; he had previously held the same billets from April 1935 to December 1936.
§ Captain T. De Witt Carr, USN, was the top-ranking officer assigned specifically to the naval training station.

an academy man.* There were maybe half a dozen or so other academy people, and I was put right into recruit training.

Paul Stillwell: What sort of an organization existed there? You showed me a picture yesterday that showed four men clustered around Commander Armstrong.† How did that fit together?

Mr. Richmond: Well, that didn't happen till six months after I reported there. So that I had six months of training with the white recruits. There were no colored recruits until, say, July of '42. In the meantime, the station was expanding at just an unbelievable rate. I would say there were probably just two recruit training regiments at the beginning of 1942. When I left the station in '44, there were close to 40 regiments.

It was in the summer of '42 that the Negro was accepted for general ratings in the Navy, and a special regiment was developed to take care of them at a new camp built to the west of the regular station.‡ It was part of the station, but these barracks where we went in at Camp Robert Smalls didn't even exist when I went there in January of '42.§ And they were finishing up building the new camp six months later: barracks, recreation hall, drill hall, and so forth.

You asked about the organization. There was a special officer assigned to take care of the Negro regiment, and he was Daniel Armstrong, class of 1915.** And then there were just four other officers assigned to help him develop Camp Robert Smalls. They were Donald Van Ness, who was the next senior under Armstrong; Vance Kauffold, an ensign; John Dille, an ensign; and then myself, Paul Richmond, an ensign.††

---

* Lieutenant Commander Harold B. Edgar, USN.
† When recruit training for black men was initiated at Great Lakes in mid-1942, the officer in charge was Lieutenant Commander Daniel W. Armstrong, USNR.
‡ Enlistment of blacks in the Navy's general service ratings began in June 1942, so they were no longer restricted to being cooks and messmen.
§ Camp Robert Smalls was named for an escaped slave who captured the Confederate steamer *Planter* during the Civil War and turned her over to the U.S. Navy. He served as pilot of the *Planter* and later of the gunboat *Keokuk*.
** After being graduated from the Naval Academy in 1915, Armstrong served on active duty through World War I and then resigned his regular commission in 1919 to pursue a civilian career. He was recalled to active duty as a lieutenant shortly before the beginning of World War II.
†† Lieutenant (junior grade) Donald O. Van Ness, USNR; Ensign Vance A. Kauffold, USNR; Ensign John F. Dille Jr., USNR. Dille's memoir is part of the Naval Institute's oral history program.

These four officers I just mentioned were each assigned a battalion. So we had a regiment and a regimental commander and four battalion commanders and empty barracks to go along with them.

Paul Stillwell: How did you four happen to be chosen—do you know?

Mr. Richmond: No, I don't. I just heard through the grapevine that they were talking about assigning officers that had been successful and they thought that would be able to do the job. And they had said in the beginning that they would all be Naval Academy men. But there weren't that many academy men to go around. Some of the ones who had been thought of to be officers there at the battalion received their orders to other assignments. One was Robert Blackwell from the class of '39.[*] He got an assignment to sea duty, and I think it was Dille that replaced him. Vance Kauffold was not an academy man either. But he was senior to me; he had come through the Naval Reserve at, I believe, the University of Illinois.

Paul Stillwell: Was that an assignment that you accepted willingly?

Mr. Richmond: Oh, yes. It was just an assignment, and I really thought it would be quite a challenge and very interesting. I never regretted it.

Paul Stillwell: What sorts of steps did you have to go through to go from no barracks to a full-fledged program in a short time?

Mr. Richmond: Well, we just turned to, and, of course, we knew how the regiments were running on the main side of Great Lakes. And, to a great extent, we followed that routine. But Commander Armstrong was a very innovative officer, a great deal of imagination. And, you know, his father had started the Hampton Institute for the

---

[*] Ensign Robert E. Blackwell, USNR.

Negroes, and Dan Armstrong himself had a great sympathy for their cause.* And so we just developed any number of interesting programs.

Paul Stillwell: What examples do you recall of the imagination?

Mr. Richmond: Well, we tried to outfit our camp with as many practical training devices as we could think of. I remember we had a 5-inch gun moved into the drill hall so that the recruits could see what a gun was like. We had classrooms set up to teach the signal flags. We had gunnery drills with a gun loader machine that they could practice on. We built an obstacle course that really was the pride of Great Lakes station.

When President Roosevelt came to visit the camp in the latter part of '42, he really spent most of his time while he was at Great Lakes visiting our camp and observing these innovations that we had there.† We ran some recruits through the obstacle course for him and so forth.

Paul Stillwell: Were the facilities at Camp Robert Smalls comparable to those on main side?

Mr. Richmond: They were absolutely comparable, and—in my opinion—better.

Paul Stillwell: In what ways?

Mr. Richmond: Well, like the obstacle course that I just mentioned. Just things that we put up. I was living in the BOQ on the main side, and a great many of my friends who also lived there were running white regiments or were in them as battalion officers.‡ We exchanged notes, and if one fellow got a good idea—like someone built models of ships—that idea was shared. The recruits could go aboard these wooden models and

---

* Brigadier General Samuel Chapman Armstrong (1839-1893) had served as colonel of a black regiment in the Civil War, and that led to his interest in vocational education for black students. In 1868 he founded the Hampton Normal and Agricultural Institute at Hampton, Virginia.
† Franklin D. Roosevelt was President of the United States from 1933 to 1945. He visited the Great Lakes Naval Training Station in mid-September 1942.
‡ BOQ – bachelor officers' quarters.

visualize where different parts of the ship were located. All kinds of metal were restricted, so practically everything was made of wood, even the beams in the drill hall and so forth.

Paul Stillwell: Was the curriculum at Camp Robert Smalls comparable to that for the white sailors?

Mr. Richmond: Yes. Of course, you've got to remember that at this time—from the middle of '42 and into '43—our primary concern was getting the recruits through their basic requirements and out to the fleet. And so there were many things that had to be done, like getting them vaccinated, dental examinations, getting them their uniforms, assigning them their service numbers, and issuing their dog tags, and getting their records set up. All this took a minimum of three weeks. The original recruit training program, I think, at one time had been three months. Then it was cut down to two months or eight weeks. Still later, I remember putting many companies through in three weeks so we could get them out to the fleet. You don't do a lot of curriculum educational training under that basis.

Paul Stillwell: I've heard that a remedial reading program was set up for some of the black recruits. What are your recollections of that?

Mr. Richmond: Well, that is true. I think that that was a development that came along after the period I just mentioned when we were sending them out in three weeks. We got back to an eight-week program in the latter part of '43.

Paul Stillwell: I'd be interested in more on Commander Armstrong and his role and the qualities in him that you recall.

Mr. Richmond: I can remember writing home to my mother that he was certainly the best officer that I had ever run into up until that time. And I guess that takes in all the ones that were at the Naval Academy when I was going through the training. So he was a very outstanding man and, as I said, very imaginative and an inspirational leader. He was working there all the time. I don't know whether he was divorced or a widower, but he was not married. And so he had the time to be there at the regiment, and he was.

He was also quite an athletic man, and he worked out regularly in the drill hall, playing badminton and volleyball with the black athletes that were there. At the station we just had an amazing array of great athletes who were coming into the Navy at that time, both black and white. Graham Martin was an outstanding colored athlete that was there at that time, and on the main side we had people like Mickey Cochrane from the Detroit Tigers and Tony Hinkle, Paul Brown.* You name them.

Paul Stillwell: From what you say, it sounds as if Armstrong was sincere in his effort to make Camp Robert Smalls succeed.

Mr. Richmond: Oh, no question about that. I give him about 102%.

Paul Stillwell: Any other examples you remember of his leadership?

Mr. Richmond: He participated in the program in every way possible. For instance, he attended the reviews weekly. When the men graduated, he was there to pass out a diploma and honor certificate to the most outstanding recruit in each company. When we had happy hour entertainment programs, he always attended and generally had a few remarks for the men.

We were taking in all kinds of men, you know, so we had not only outstanding athletes, but there were outstanding musicians and men of culture that were there, literary people. He had them writing scripts for plays, and we developed just an excellent choir. The blacks are great at singing. We had a leader who had a doctorate in music from some university. His name was Elmer Hathcock, and he was the head of the music

---

* Graham Edward Martin was a member of the Golden Thirteen, the first group of black naval officers. His oral history is in the Naval Institute collection. Lieutenant Gordon S. Cochrane, USNR, had been a star catcher and manager of the Detroit Tigers; he is a member of the baseball hall of fame. Lieutenant Paul D. Hinkle, USNR, is a member of the basketball hall of fame; he was for many years head coach of football, basketball, and baseball at Butler University in Indianapolis. Lieutenant Paul Brown, USNR, later achieved fame in professional football as head coach of the Cleveland Browns.

department. It was considered a great privilege by the whites to come over and listen to some of our happy hour shows.

Plus which, we were having prominent Negro talent come to the station. I can remember that Marian Anderson gave a concert, and Hazel Scott came.* Marva Barrow, the wife of Joe Louis, attended some of our functions and presented awards to the men.† There was something going on all the time. He kept the pot stirred up.

Paul Stillwell: Well, it sounds like he was doing a lot to foster morale.

Mr. Richmond: He was.

Paul Stillwell: Did he use his clout to go to the white hierarchy and get things for Camp Robert Smalls?

Mr. Richmond: Yes, I would say he did everything he possibly could. I remember one time I was listening to him on the phone while he was talking. The fellow on the other end of the line apparently had said "No."

He said, "I think we're going to have to settle this on the phone. Let's be reasonable. Or am I going to have to come over there and make you do it?"

Paul Stillwell: Sounds like a forceful individual.

Mr. Richmond: He was forceful but gentlemanly.

Paul Stillwell: Yesterday you used the term in describing him that he was a "can-do officer."

---

* Marian Anderson was a noted concert contralto; Hazel Scott was a pianist who later married U.S. Representative Adam Clayton Powell.
† Joseph Louis Barrow (1914-1981) fought under the name Joe Louis. He won the boxing heavyweight championship in 1936 and successfully defended the title 25 times before retiring in 1949. A later comeback attempt failed.

Mr. Richmond: Absolutely. And, as 90% of us did, he went overseas later on. He was over in Hawaii, and I was over there with him part of that time. Jack Dille was there, and, oh, just a great number of our officers.

As I showed you last night, there were just five officers who started the program. Then I showed you that picture where in one year's time there must have been, let's say, 40 commissioned officers and maybe 100 white chiefs and some black chiefs.

Paul Stillwell: Now did these white chiefs run the individual companies in the battalions?

Mr. Richmond: Yes, they did. They were, for the most part, a group of young college men who had been successful athletes in their colleges but not graduates. And they had been recruited by Gene Tunney.[*] And, as a matter of fact, they picked up the nickname "Tunney fish," or they were called "Tunney chiefs." There is actually a tunny fish, and the old-line Navy chiefs knew about this, and they labeled these new young fellows the "Tunney fish."

They had been promised that they would get commissions directly after coming in as chiefs. It didn't work out that way. I can remember two years later on, they still hadn't received their commissions. It was a little bit of a problem when the candidates for the black officers were announced, and some of them realized that these brand-new black people were going to be commissioned ahead of them.

Paul Stillwell: So there was some resentment of the black officer candidates?

Mr. Richmond: A little healthy, I think, resentment. I don't ever recall anything particularly glaring.

---

[*] Lieutenant Commander James J. "Gene" Tunney, USNR, was the boxing heavyweight champion from 1926 to 1928. During World War II, he was in charge of the Navy's program of athletic instruction. The men he recruited were given direct appointments as chief petty officer specialists.

Paul Stillwell: Did you have any problem in that these Tunney chiefs did not have a lot of Navy background and experience, and yet they were trying to teach the recruits about the Navy?

Mr. Richmond: This was true all around. That's why the Naval Academy men were actually spread so thin. And, of course, most of the academy men were out in the fleet, so those of us ashore were really in a minority. During the first six months when I was at Great Lakes, one of my first jobs was to indoctrinate the white officers that were coming into the service. And so I gave them lectures on gunnery and seamanship and naval organization and so forth. Most of those officers became battalion commanders on the white side and also regimental commanders.

We had some outstanding men from civilian life, like Jack Dille, who was one of them. He came in at that same time. He'd had a military training in college. Many of these other men did too. I remember Lou Hager had been in the Army Reserve and had even had duty at West Point.* I don't know how that got him a Navy commission, but it was because of his previous military training.

Paul Stillwell: Who did you have as the instructors in the individual courses to teach Navy subjects to the recruits?

Mr. Richmond: There were some black chiefs there who had been in the Navy. And, as Jack Dille remarked in his interview, they all had what were called left-arm rates, such as machinist's mate.† We had maybe a dozen of those men. They all pitched in on teaching, and we did have some other old-line white chiefs, who were training the new chiefs as well. That's the way it worked.

---

* Lieutenant Louis A. Hager, Jr., USNR.
† During World War II and before, petty officers in the deck ratings—such as boatswain's mate, quartermaster, and signalman—took pride in their ratings' long-traditional status in the Navy by wearing their rating badges on their right sleeves. Petty officers in the other ratings wore the insignia on their left sleeves.

Mr. Paul D. Richmond Interview (1/14/90) – Page 11

Paul Stillwell: Well, and it would help if you've got a pretty standardized curriculum. I guess you take the new chiefs through that, and then they, in turn, pass on what they have learned.

Mr. Richmond: We had a system that was called "shadowing." The new man shadowed the older man, the man with the more experience, by following him around and watching what he did. After six months or a year, as we got into the program, the new men were shadowing somebody who had been shadowing somebody else just three to six months previously.

Paul Stillwell: What are your recollections of the other three individuals that served as the battalion commanders: Kauffold, Van Ness, and Dille?

Mr. Richmond: Just the finest fellows that I can think of. They're all good friends of mine. We got along marvelously.

Paul Stillwell: What individual recollections do you have of them?

Mr. Richmond: Donald Van Ness was a Naval Academy man. He was about the same age as Jack Dille. They were both approximately seven years older than I; I'd say that made them 28 at this time.[*] Jack had been in business as a newspaperman. His family owned a newspaper syndicate. I don't know whether you knew this or not—his father invented Buck Rogers.[†]

Paul Stillwell: No, I don't remember that.

Mr. Richmond: That was one of the things he was known for around the base. Van Ness had gotten out of the service and had had some business experience in St. Louis, and he

---

[*] Van Ness and Dille were born in 1913; Richmond was born in 1920.
[†] John F. Dille, president of the National Newspaper Service of Chicago, created in 1929 a comic strip titled "Buck Rogers in the 25th Century." It featured interplanetary warfare and communications and employed futuristic weapons such as death rays and rocket pistols. Dille developed the concept for the strip and supplied story ideas; the artist was Richard W. Calkins.

had more rank than the rest of us, because he was older and had graduated in 1935 from the academy. Vance Kauffold was quite an outstanding athlete in his own right, a basketball and football player. He had been a teacher in a school system in Illinois. As I say, we were very close and saw a lot of each other.

Paul Stillwell: Did you meet regularly with Commander Armstrong? Daily? What was the arrangement there?

Mr. Richmond: Well, we met a lot with him. We had many staff meetings. I couldn't say whether they were on a daily basis, but they were pretty often. And he was perpetually coming up with new things that he wanted to do. Like, he installed an E award at Camp Robert Smalls before any of the white regiments had such an award. And then it was copied in the white camps, and I have pictures of awarding this E flag for excellence to the outstanding company. He had somebody compose a creed of loyalty for the blacks, which they all recited at graduation time and signed a paper and were given this sheet to take with them as a memento of their training. That was never adopted in the white training on the main side.

Paul Stillwell: Were there any problems that you recall that had to be solved because the blacks had not had this experience before in the general service ratings?

Mr. Richmond: My chief recollection, Paul, is that, as far as the Navy was concerned, the blacks had no different problems than the whites had. The whites were just as upset and felt as strange about coming into the training program as the blacks. The blacks just didn't know that the whites were experiencing exactly the same things that they were. Of course, in the case of the whites there could be no charge of racial discrimination. But fundamentally the problems were the same. We treated the blacks just like we treated the whites.

Paul Stillwell: So you're saying it was a matter of the culture shock of coming into the Navy?

Mr. Richmond: I think that was about 95% of it.

Paul Stillwell: You described also an interesting experience you had going on shore patrol. If you could put that on the record, please.

Mr. Richmond: Well, I had been doing shore patrol right from the first day, I guess, that I got there at the station—being the junior, junior ensign. And so I had taken white shore patrols to Waukegan and Milwaukee and occasionally to Chicago. We did this even though Chicago had its own white shore patrol down there, so it wasn't part of our responsibility. Eventually there developed a professional shore patrol that was practically like a police force. Our new black regiment necessitated another requirement. When we did finally give liberty to the recruits who had finished their training and were free to go on liberty, we ran a train down to the south side of Chicago for them. I went on the first all-black shore patrol the weekend of that liberty.

The interesting thing that I was telling you about was that I had a regular black chief from the old Navy who went along with me. On the train ride down, he said, "When we get there, I'm going to introduce you to 'The Man.' 'The Man' will take care of you." And that's all he told me. So when we arrived in the south side of Chicago, we turned the men loose and established our patrol. The men were patrolling around the streets and going in and looking at the bars and so forth.

After a while, this chief said, "Come on. We'll meet 'The Man.'" So we went over to a nightclub that was called the Cotton Club. We were ushered right in, and this chief seemed to know the people there very well. The next thing I knew, I was in the back office, and we walked in. And there was "The Man." It was Joe Louis, the famous Negro boxer. I guess I don't have to identify him for you. I was introduced to him, and the chief said, "The lieutenant here is in charge of the shore patrol, and he wants to have things run properly."

Joe Louis said, "I'll tell you what, Lieutenant. If you have any trouble, you just come to me. There ain't going to be any trouble." And there wasn't.

Paul Stillwell: What do you recall in general about the disciplinary situation in Camp Robert Smalls?

Mr. Richmond: I would say that it was probably no better or worse than on the white side. We had a disciplinary organization that was called the slackers' squad. People that did cause trouble were assigned to this slackers' squad and given extra physical instruction, which turned out to be in the form of boxing lessons with some pretty good boxers. And, by and large, the majority didn't want to be assigned to the slackers' squad.

Paul Stillwell: So that was some good incentive to get along with the program.

Mr. Richmond: Right.

Paul Stillwell: After a time and you had graduated a number of the black recruits, did you keep some of them on to help administer the program?

Mr. Richmond: Absolutely. I didn't have much to do with that selection. That was done by Commander Armstrong in his regimental office. And one of the black recruits later became the yeoman for Lieutenant Dille, and that was Reginald Goodwin.[*] And he was later selected as one of the candidates for the officer candidate school.

And there were a good many other colored ratings that came along. And then, eventually, we organized our own service school, right there at Camp Robert Smalls. I would say it was probably towards the end of 1943 that we opened up two more regiments to accommodate the influx of recruits. And so, having started out with one, we now had two recruit regiments, and the 18th regiment housed the service school.

Paul Stillwell: Why was Camp Robert Smalls expanded, rather than integrating the blacks and the whites in their training at some point?

---

[*] Reginald Ernest Goodwin was a member of the Golden Thirteen. He died before he could be interviewed as part of the Naval Institute's oral history program.

Mr. Richmond: That was just the Navy policy. I would say that maintaining the segregated setup was the wish of Commander Armstrong. He certainly wanted it that way, and it was his baby. He was happy the way it was running.

Paul Stillwell: In picking the white chiefs that served with the black companies, was there any screening to see whether their attitudes were sympathetic to the blacks?

Mr. Richmond: I never did any of it. I don't know whether it was done or not. As I recall, it was very much like Jack Dille described it, that if we ran into somebody that didn't measure up to our standards and, let's say, was antagonistic or whatnot, he was relieved of his duty and sent elsewhere. We didn't try to force this duty on them, although we did have any number of southern chiefs there who were very amenable to the program.

Paul Stillwell: But only if it wouldn't be known back home, probably, what they were doing.

Mr. Richmond: There was that. Yes, I remember an occasion when Dorothy Donegan came to put on a concert one time.* I invited this one chief that was from down in Louisiana someplace. I said, "Come on, let's have dinner with Dorothy Donegan."

He said, "Not on your life. If a picture was ever taken of me having dinner with her, my name would be mud. I couldn't go home."

I said, "Well, come on. There'll be no pictures." And there weren't, and he did come. I think that a great deal of racial barriers were broken down that way. And when the whole thing was over, we had a better country for it.

Paul Stillwell: That's because they were dealing with people as individuals, rather than as stereotypes.

Mr. Richmond: I think that's right.

---

* Dorothy Donegan was a popular black singer and pianist.

Paul Stillwell: You showed me an article last night that you wrote with the intention of submitting to the *Naval Institute Proceedings* on the blacks in the Navy at that point.* It suggests that you had developed considerable enthusiasm for the program by that time.

Mr. Richmond: That's right. I did write such an article, and I showed it to you. It describes the training that we had there. I submitted it through channels, and the recruit training officer called me in and wanted to know why I was writing such an article and what was so special about the blacks. He made several comments that he didn't think we needed this extra publicity.

Of course, we were getting excellent publicity, as I mentioned, when President Roosevelt came. He devoted so much time just to the black regiment. I think there was a little jealousy on the part of the whites, an attitude of, "Why make such a thing out of it?" We were just trying to do our duty, our job, our assignment. And, of course, when I wrote the article, I was actually looking for recognition of the job we had done. And I thought it might alert the fleet that these fellows were being trained for regular assignments, that they were no longer just mess boys.

Paul Stillwell: What was the rest of the story on the article? It didn't get published. You said you were discouraged from submitting it.

Mr. Richmond: Well, yes I was. I was told, "You can send it in to the Institute if you want to, but we advise against it." I wrote home to my mother that I lost the argument, but I thought it was more prudent to go along with their thinking than raise a ruckus when it wasn't absolutely necessary.

Paul Stillwell: Did any stories come back to the camp about exploits of black sailors once they'd gotten into the fleet that you could use as good examples?

---

* Richmond wrote a letter, dated 25 March 1943, asking for approval of the article by the chain of command.

Mr. Richmond: No, I don't really remember too many. In that article I wrote for the Institute, I did mention a Negro named Dorie Miller who had been a mess boy at Pearl Harbor during the attack there.[*] He performed gallantly and was awarded the Navy Cross. So I cited that as an example, and I think we used to tell the recruits about it, that he was outstanding. No reason why they shouldn't measure up in every way.

Paul Stillwell: How much advance warning did you get on the program to train black officer candidates?

Mr. Richmond: Not much. Not any more than I did when I was first assigned to the black regiment. And I don't know that it was held back or anything. I think they moved ahead as quickly as they could. I think by that time Commander Armstrong was dealing with the Bureau of Personnel in Washington quite a bit. And Van Ness had been sent to Washington as well. When he left, I was made the commanding officer of the regiment. So really the training of the black candidates fell kind of naturally to me, and I still had this other training. And, of course, at that time I was the only one who had been to Annapolis that was there for it. So I enjoyed the challenge.

Paul Stillwell: Would you say you had perhaps a month lead time before the officer training began?

Mr. Richmond: No more than that certainly. I think Commander Armstrong just told me, "We've got these candidates selected." I had nothing to do with the selection, and I don't to this day know the particulars of how they were selected. To my recollection, out of the 13, at least ten had gone through Camp Robert Smalls for basic training. And what we tried to do was to set up a program that would parallel the program for the so-called 90-day wonders that were trained at Columbia and other universities.[†]

---

[*] Mess Attendant Doris Miller, USN, was on board the battleship *West Virginia* (BB-48) on 7 December 1941. He manned an antiaircraft machine gun and fired at attacking Japanese planes. He was lost in the sinking of the escort carrier *Liscome Bay* (CVE-56) in November 1943. The USS *Miller* (DE-1091), commissioned in 1973, was named for him.

[†] Under the V-7 program, volunteers with sufficient secondary education—typically, bachelor's degrees—were trained as Naval Reserve officers for surface ships.

Paul Stillwell: Where did you get the curriculum that you used?

Mr. Richmond: I just made it up actually from remembering my own training. You see, I was only two years out of the Naval Academy, and what I tried to do was to give the officer candidates just an abbreviated course in the subjects that we had studied at Annapolis in a professional way. Nearly all of these men were college graduates to start out with. I gave them U.S. Navy 101. I selected subjects like seamanship, navigation, gunnery, naval regulations, naval law. We took them to the rifle range, and we had an antiaircraft simulator that we used to fire.

Paul Stillwell: Could you describe in a little more detail what the antiaircraft simulator was like?

Mr. Richmond: Well, it was housed in a small building that would hold maybe 50 men, and it ran movies of planes attacking a ship. It was not unlike the little mechanical shooting galleries that you see in the amusement parks, only on a much larger scale. At the rear of the building they had a simulated antiaircraft gun that you could point at these targets on the screen. If you were on the target, a buzzer rang, and if you weren't on the target, it didn't ring.

Paul Stillwell: Do you recall any shooting with actual antiaircraft guns?*

Mr. Richmond: Oh, no.
There was an interesting thing that happened with Gordon Buhrer, my roommate from the Naval Academy, who came to visit me.† He'd been the gunnery officer on a destroyer and participated in the landing at North Africa. He was sitting in watching this

---

* In the oral histories of the Golden Thirteen members, a few did provide recollections of antiaircraft practice with real guns rather than simulators.
† Lieutenant (junior grade) Gordon C. Buhrer, USN. As an ensign he had been assigned to USS *Ludlow* (DD-438) during the Allied invasion of North Africa in November 1942.

thing, and some of the chiefs who were conducting the class said, "Would you like to take a shot at it, Lieutenant?"

And he said, "I'd love to." So he got up, and they ran the planes by him, and he shot a couple of times here and there, and the buzzer rang.

And they said, "Hang on it, there. You're doing great."

And he didn't particularly hold the trigger down. Finally he said, "Well, that's enough."

They said, "You could have been on that buzzer all the time with your ability."

He said, "I'll tell you a couple of things. If you were swinging a gun around and firing the way you fellows are doing it, you'd shoot down all the rigging on your ship. Plus which, you heat up the gun barrel, and it would jam on you. And, thirdly, that plane ain't going to fly no more anyway." So he got kind of a kick out of it, and the men appreciated the input from someone who had actually been there.

Paul Stillwell: How did you pick the instructors for the individual subjects?

Mr. Richmond: We took the men that were best qualified for it. We had lawyers there who were in the legal department, and they taught the subjects in naval regulations and law. I taught the classes in navigation and gunnery, because I figured I was the most qualified. Then Lieutenant Dille, as he has pointed out in his interview, was more of a morale officer and a counselor for them, and he really spent more time individually with the men. He doesn't quite remember how he got assigned to it, but that was his job, and he did an excellent job at it. It wasn't my job to do that, I didn't feel, and I never did socialize with them or fraternize. I didn't think it was proper for a schoolteacher to be in that capacity.

Paul Stillwell: Was this viewed as an experiment—to see whether blacks could become officers?

Mr. Richmond: I didn't think it was an experiment. It was a fact. We were making them officers. The assignment was, "Train them, and they're going to be commissioned." I personally tried to make it as difficult for them as I possibly could so that they would get the best training. If I might have scared them a little bit that they weren't going to make it, it was on purpose—a way of motivating them. I had no particular intentions of purposely flunking anybody. I personally thought that they all were going to make it. There was a great divergence of ability and previous training, so that some of them learned some things faster than others. And others were stronger in another phase.

Paul Stillwell: The individuals that I've interviewed have made the point that at night they blocked out the light from their barracks. They would study in the head after they were supposed to be in bed. I take it you really didn't have that much objection to them studying together.

Mr. Richmond: No, I had no objection. I just wanted them to learn the material. I think that was great, if they were helping each other. I wasn't aware of the extent that they may have stayed up, but we did that at the Naval Academy too.

Paul Stillwell: So it wouldn't have bothered you had you found out they were staying up past taps?

Mr. Richmond: No way would it bother me.

Paul Stillwell: In fact, you may have been impressed by their motivation.

Mr. Richmond: I was.

Paul Stillwell: I've got a list of the individuals, and I'd like to run through it please and just see what memories you have of the members of the group.

Mr. Richmond: Well, I'd like to say this, Paul. With a few exceptions, like, say, with Graham Martin, whom I probably knew the best of the whole group, I can't give you a lot of individual recollections. They were all nice fellows. They were clean and bright, serious. I guess I can remember that Dennis Nelson was a little bit more of a cutup and more gregarious than some of the others, and some were more reserved.* But I don't think I could really give you person-by-person qualities of each individual man.

Paul Stillwell: Well, what do you recall of Dennis Nelson? What specifics on his cutting up?

Mr. Richmond: I don't remember any specific things. If you want to talk about this, the Graham Martin incident is the one that stands out the most in my mind. And it was really a very serious incident, where he was shadowing a white company commander. During a Saturday inspection they discovered one of the recruits that had a package of cigarettes in his blouse pocket, which was wrong, of course. And the chief pulled the package out of his pocket and gave it to Martin and said, "Make him eat these," which was a ridiculous disciplinary tactic that he thought might impress somebody. I don't know how.

In any case, Graham Martin was a fine athlete and an intelligent man that had been trained in physical education, and he knew what the damage would be. And he said, "There's no way I'm going to do that."

And the chief said, "You either do it, or you're on report." And he was put on report for failing to carry out an order. This was reported to me as the regimental commander, so I called Graham in. I said, "From what I have heard, you did the right thing. I don't blame you, and I wouldn't have made the man eat them either. I think it's ridiculous. Let's forget the whole thing." And I didn't discipline the chief either. I took the attitude of, "Instead of looking for problems, let's ignore it."

But the chief didn't ignore it. He told some people on the main side of the camp. The next thing I knew, Commander Armstrong had been called over to explain what kind of an outfit he was running over there, where the Negro candidates weren't obeying orders? Well, I think he changed his mind when he heard the circumstances of the orders, but, in any case, Commander Armstrong called me in and said that he had to discipline me in some way for not being more positive. And so he asked me to write an

---

* Dennis Denmark Nelson II was a member of the Golden Thirteen, the only one of the group who completed a full career in the Navy. He died before he could be interviewed for the Naval Institute's oral history program.

essay on what I had learned at the academy about following orders. And I think I told you last night that I gave an illustration about the manner in which Admiral Nelson followed out a few orders.* And Commander Armstrong accepted that as my explanation, and the whole matter was dropped.

Paul Stillwell: Well, you cited a case that's become quite famous--that when Admiral Nelson was given an order to withdraw from battle by signals, he put his telescope to his blind eye so he didn't see the signal.

Mr. Richmond: That's absolutely right. And one of his most famous cases, too, he was told to follow in a line in the battle and turn his ship to starboard. And instead of turning to starboard, he broke out of the line, turned to port, went down, crossed the T, and it became one of the most famous naval operations in history.

Paul Stillwell: So the matter essentially ended with that essay on Nelson?

Mr. Richmond: That's right, as far as I was concerned. I understand that Graham remembers the whole incident, too, pretty well.

Paul Stillwell: Yes, he does.

Mr. Richmond: I have never seen any of these men since they graduated. As you know, I have that lovely picture of 12 of them—and it's signed by each one of them—in my scrapbook. And I guess it was William White that was not present.†

---

* Lord Horatio Viscount Nelson (1758-1805), British naval hero of the Battle of Cape St. Vincent, 1797, Battle of the Nile, 1798, Trafalgar, 1805. In the 1801 Battle of Copenhagen his superior, Admiral Sir Hyde Parker gave Nelson the discretion to withdraw in a message sent by signal flags. Nelson disobeyed the order and succeeded in destroying many enemy ships. He quipped that he didn't see the order because he put the telescope to his blind eye.

† William Sylvester White was a member of the Golden Thirteen; his oral history is in the Naval Institute' collection. When the initial photo of the first black naval officers was taken in March 1944, White was missing because he was having dental work done. A subsequent photo, including all 13, was taken for the *Life* magazine issue of 24 April 1944.

Paul Stillwell: Right.

Mr. Richmond: I have corresponded with some of them after they got the publicity on going aboard the destroyer *Kidd* at their reunion.* I just read about it in the paper, and when I did see it, I was so interested that they were down there, I called the base and found out what was going on and talked to them on the phone. And that was the time I corresponded with a number of them.

Paul Stillwell: You were telling me also you had a conversation with somebody, and you were just extolling Martin and how impressed you were by him as an individual.

Mr. Richmond: Absolutely. I guess, as you know, he was an Indiana University graduate, and he had a master's degree as well. And I was under the impression—somebody had told me that he was a Phi Beta Kappa student. I don't know whether that's true or not, but I had heard that. And then for him to be able to play on the Great Lakes varsity football team was, in my opinion, great.†

We talked about the athletics of the regiment, and our opinion was that it was to train the men for physical ability and recreation as well. We wanted to organize our own teams and compete. The black athletes in Camp Robert Smalls won almost every time they competed. I think we were right at the top of the whole camp. We had a meeting of black leaders that were mostly newspaper people, and Adam Clayton Powell came out to attend this conference.‡ This must have been about the time the officers were being commissioned. It was early '44, as I recall. And the training program at Great Lakes was winding down to some extent.

The Negro personalities that were attending at that time seemed to think that the Navy should do something about breaking the color barrier in sports—for baseball, as an

---

* From 13 to 15 April 1982, the nine surviving members of the Golden Thirteen held a reunion on board the guided missile destroyer *Kidd* (DDG-993) at sea in the Atlantic. See PH2 Drake White, "Golden 13 Together Again," *All Hands*, August 1982, pages 8-11.
† Martin discussed his football experiences in some detail in his own oral history.
‡ Adam Clayton Powell, Jr., was a flamboyant black U.S. Representative from New York City. In 1945 he appointed to the Naval Academy Wesley Brown, Jr., who in 1949 became the first black man to graduate from the academy.

example.* They would like to have had just one of our people playing on the white team, as opposed to having an all-black team. Because they said later on, when the war was over, they could use this as a lever, saying that they had played during the war, and why couldn't they play now? But while I was there, none of that was done. Shortly after I left the program, I guess they finally did integrate the training, that is, integrate the blacks with the whites. Camp Robert Smalls was more or less disbanded.

Paul Stillwell: Were you aware of people other than perhaps this chief who gave the order about eating cigarettes, people who did not want the black officer candidates to succeed?

Mr. Richmond: I don't really remember anybody like that.

Paul Stillwell: So he would be really an exceptional case?

Mr. Richmond: Very much an exception, extremely.

Paul Stillwell: Some of the black officers whom I talked to felt that the instructors in the classes were condescending. Others didn't get that reaction at all. Was this kind of a thing, the approach, something that you ever discussed with the instructors?

Mr. Richmond: Well, I didn't think any of them were condescending. I certainly didn't go to them and say, "Don't be condescending."

Paul Stillwell: And you wouldn't have any sort of feedback that would indicate at the time whether they were or weren't?

Mr. Richmond: No. I was thinking in my own mind and comparing it with when I was at the Naval Academy. And you have all different kinds of instructors at the academy.

---

* Professional baseball was not integrated until the 1946 season when Jackie Robinson played for a minor league farm team of the Brooklyn Dodgers. He joined the major league Dodgers in 1947.

Some were excellent, and some weren't too good. And I suppose in our school at Great Lakes we had some that were excellent, and there may have been some that weren't too good. We didn't assign them a bum instructor on purpose—I'll tell you that. We were trying to assign the best that we had.

Paul Stillwell: What do you remember about your own classroom experiences with the group?

Mr. Richmond: Well, just pretty much that they were very serious. We'd have question-and-answer sessions. And I based the training pretty much on what I'd experienced at Annapolis. And, you know, at Annapolis we got a quiz every day and a grade, and I think the same thing applied there in my classes. Now maybe in some of the other classes that some of the other teachers had they didn't do it that way because they had gone to civilian colleges and whatnot. But I think I gave them a quiz at the end of every program and gave them a grade. And I know that they were all graded on their class performance. Those grades were sent to Washington, and I've heard that they were pretty much in keeping—and maybe a little bit better than the average white grade. I don't know what that proves, and I don't have any of the records now, so I couldn't even tell you if one was exceptionally higher than another.

Paul Stillwell: Was there any interest expressed from Washington from time to time on how these men were doing?

Mr. Richmond: Not to me. They might have very well to Armstrong.

Paul Stillwell: The Naval Academy took three and a half years to turn you into a naval officer. How did you decide what out of those three-plus years to compress into three months for these officer candidates?

Mr. Richmond: It was just a matter of a personal opinion, I guess. I tried to think of things that would be of value to them. We didn't teach too many of the specific things. Like we didn't try to teach them how to signal between ships and things like that.

In the navigation course I used a civilian version of Dutton, *The Primer of Navigation* by George W. Mixter, which had been published to help yachtsmen and whatnot.* I thought it would be easier for them to tackle this when they only had such a short time. We taught them basic navigating and, oh, like the points of the compass and dead reckoning.† I can remember we had sextants in the room that I was able to get from the main side to show them how star sights were taken and gave them a description. But I don't think that we really ever taught them to work out a star sight program. We showed them what the problem was, but, like you say, I took navigation for a whole year trying to learn what it was all about. And it's not an easy subject to grasp for the uninitiated.

Paul Stillwell: Did you have any practical works or exercises in the classroom in things like coastal piloting?

Mr. Richmond: Yes, but nothing outside of the classroom.

Paul Stillwell: Was there any attempt to foster competition within the class, as the Naval Academy had fostered competition?

Mr. Richmond: What kind of competition?

Paul Stillwell: At the academy class standing is very important.

Mr. Richmond: No, no. I would say we shied away from that. It was a group effort. It was my hope that they all pass. And I wasn't trying to have one fellow be ahead of the

---

* *Dutton's Navigation and Piloting* is a standard textbook on the subject, now in its 15th edition. It began in 1926 as *Navigation and Nautical Astronomy*, written by Commander Benjamin Dutton, USN.
† Dead reckoning, taken from "deduced reckoning," is a method by which the course and speed are plotted from the last known position to arrive at a deduction concerning the new position.

others. No way. There were only 13 or 14 or whatever there were, I guess.* It was a small group.

I've heard that they felt that they were confined in a small area. They were, I guess, but it wasn't to put a hardship on them. That was all the space we had. All the rest of the training was going on. This was in addition. We had the full service school there. They weren't supposed to mingle with the service school people. And we had the recruits there, and they weren't supposed to mingle with the recruits. That sort of necessitated them being confined to their barracks and schoolroom. And they were. And they were supposed to be there studying. My God, they were supposed to learn all this technical detail in a very short time. And it probably was tough on them, for they were older. All of these men were older than I was, and perhaps more experienced.†

Paul Stillwell: The classroom, from what I've heard, was right there in that same barracks, so that the instructors came to them.

Mr. Richmond: That's right.

Paul Stillwell: Now you're saying they weren't supposed to mingle with the service school people and the recruits. Is that because they were doing something different?

Mr. Richmond: Well, I imagine that they could have mingled with them after their working hours. Like, for instance, I think everybody was free to go to a movie in the evening. It seems to me that both the service school men and the recruits were marched to the movie, which was shown in the drill hall—practically every night a movie of some kind. Because you couldn't accommodate the whole camp, certain selected companies would be marched to the movie, and then they were free to wander back to their barracks on their own and be back in time to turn in for taps.

---

* Sixteen enlisted men went through the training. Thirteen became officers, and the other three remained enlisted.
† The two youngest members of the Golden Thirteen were John W. Reagan and Frank E. Sublett, both born 5 March 1920. Paul Richmond was born 7 November 1920.

Paul Stillwell: The black officers differed in their recollections of whether they were permitted liberty or not. What do you recall on that point?

Mr. Richmond: I don't recall anything about it. There was no particular restriction against giving them liberty, and I can remember my general attitude was that I thought it was good for the morale, whether they were blacks or white. My assignment after I left the black regiment was to take over a regiment of white officers that had been dropped from the V-5 program. They were being trained as aviators, and the Navy found out that it had more aviators than it needed. So there were, I would say, close to 1,000 fellows who had already ordered their ensigns' uniforms that were turned back as first class seamen. And if you want to see a discouraged bunch of people, they were it.

Commander Turek asked me if I would take the job, and I said, "I'll only take it with certain qualifications on it. And that is that I can run it the way I want to run it."[*] I understood that I had been picked because I was about the same age as these fellows. And it turned out to be that I was not only the same age, I had gone to the same high school with some of them. And so one of the things that I wanted to give these people was a lot more liberty than they would have gotten in the normal training regiment. And they got it. So what I'm trying to illustrate is that I had nothing against people going on liberty. They could go on liberty as often as it was practical. I would have been the same way out in the fleet about liberty—in fact, I was. I can remember a few times.

Paul Stillwell: There were three of the men who went through the training with the Golden Thirteen who were not commissioned. And from our discussion yesterday it sounds as if you were not aware of why those three did not become officers.

Mr. Richmond: No, I'm not aware of the reasons. I wasn't consulted in that. I taught the class, gave them the grades, turned in the grades, and that was the extent of my responsibility.

---

[*] Commander William Turek, USNR, was recruit training officer for the entire station. Following his assignment at Camp Robert Smalls, Lieutenant Richmond had returned to the main side of the camp to train white personnel.

Paul Stillwell: Do you have any recollection of the oath-giving when they individually became ensigns?

Mr. Richmond: I wasn't there, and neither was Jack Dille, oddly enough. The reason I wasn't there was because I was on leave. I hadn't had any leave in about two years, and so I went to Florida. I was really quite tired out, to tell you the truth, after this intensive program of training the officers and writing a lot of the program. And, as you know, I wrote a lot of other things and did a chief boatswain's mate program as well. And I was just very happy to go down to Florida and lie on the beach for a while. The candidates were commissioned during that time, and, as I said, I never saw them again. I was always curious about them, and that's why when I did hear about them, I phoned right away to Norfolk.

Maybe six months or so later, I arrived in Hawaii, where Jack Dille was stationed at an ammunition camp. And then later he became a public relations officer. Dan Armstrong was out there, and I think he'd been promoted to captain by that time and was still coordinating the Negro in the fleet program. And he was helpful. The Navy personnel office was considering whether I'd be assigned to something still in the Negro program. And I expressed a desire to see some fighting, and the Negroes weren't where the fighting was going on. I think Captain Armstrong appreciated my request and probably pulled some strings which got me onto Admiral J. L. Hall's staff that went in on the Okinawa invasion on the USS *Teton*.*

Paul Stillwell: Do you remember anything of the decision that went into making Lear a warrant officer rather than an ensign?†

Mr. Richmond: It was because he didn't have a college degree. And this was the reason why those "Tunney fish" chiefs had not been given commissions, because they didn't have college degrees. And, my heavens, you know, if they had been holding out on

---

* Rear Admiral John L. Hall, USN, was Commander Task Force 55 (Southern Attack Force), embarked in the amphibious force flagship *Teton* (AGC-14) for the invasion of Okinawa in April 1945.
† Charles Byrd Lear was a member of the Golden Thirteen. He died shortly after World War II, probably a suicide.

hundreds of white guys because of this disqualification, you couldn't very well do it with the colored.

Paul Stillwell: Do you have any other specific memories of Lear?

Mr. Richmond: Just that he was a real nice fellow. No, I don't recall anything like the Graham Martin incident or whatever. That was a pretty big thing, and that's what makes Martin stand out. Plus which, I admired him so much. I really felt that he was a better man than I was. And I told a lot of people that too. I said, "You wouldn't have this racial prejudice if you really thought this fellow was superior to yourself."

And they'd say, "You don't really believe that, do you, Paul?"

And I'd say, "My God, the record looks that way. He's done a hell of a lot more than I have."

Paul Stillwell: Do you have any specific memories of Reginald Goodwin, the man who'd worked in the front office before this?

Mr. Richmond: Just as a very fine man, and I guess I would have had more contact with him, not only because I knew Lieutenant Dille, but I used to see him in the regimental office. He was a very capable, efficient person, and he got along. And there we had white yeomen, chief yeomen and so forth. All got along smoothly. We all got along. We used to eat in the same mess hall together. I guess the officers did eat in their own section of the mess hall. But we used to see them. And I used to go out with some of them, the white chiefs, to a dinner occasionally, outside the base. But mostly I stayed with the officers. That's what you're supposed to do. At the Naval Academy they taught us never to fraternize with enlisted men. But that was breaking down during World War II, and I think all throughout the service there was a lot more mixing like that.

Paul Stillwell: One thing you mentioned last night was that these black officers, once they were commissioned, were not expected to go to the officers' club. How did that come about?

Mr. Richmond: Well, it just came about naturally with the white officers. They certainly didn't want them over there. I showed you in a letter that I said I didn't think that these men would do that.* We tried to say, "For Pete's sake, you want to be successful. Now don't be bringing up a lot of things that would quash the program." And I don't think I ever told them they couldn't go there. I think I probably told them that it wouldn't be wise for them, and it would be foolish actually, because they would be jeopardizing the program.

Paul Stillwell: Because it would antagonize the white officers.

Mr. Richmond: Yes. It was sort of like the same way as the officers said to me about sending in my article to the Institute: "You know, everything you wrote there is true, Paul, but why bring it up and maybe antagonize 50% of the fleet and say what are they doing? Why are they promoting this thing?" Because it got promoted very fundamentally, as you and I both know, by Eleanor Roosevelt right from the top.† And she had a very sincere interest in breaking down the racial prejudice in the entire country.

Paul Stillwell: This same philosophy that discouraged submitting your article—would you say that was what discouraged publicity about the commissioning of these black officers?

Mr. Richmond: Possibly. I'm not aware of what publicity there was. Of course, Jack Dille would know a lot more about that, because he was a public relations officer. He was assigned to get a lot of publicity for the black sailors. He wasn't at Great Lakes at the time of the commissioning, and I don't even know how it was done, to tell you the truth.

---

* In a letter dated 1 April 1944 to a friend named Stuart MacDiarmid, Lieutenant Richmond wrote of the newly commissioned officers: "They are all good leaders and they are not radical in any sense of the word. They were picked because we knew that we could count on them to benefit the Navy and they will not raise racial issues, I am sure, such as coming to the Officers Club or anything of that nature. They are loyal to the Navy."

† Eleanor Roosevelt was the socially conscious wife of President Franklin D. Roosevelt.

Paul Stillwell: There was no effort to publicize it while they were going through the program, apparently.

Mr. Richmond: No, it was low profile.

Paul Stillwell: And I guess you mentioned last night that part of that reason was to avoid antagonizing the Tunney chiefs who weren't getting commissioned, and this would be yet another reminder.

Mr. Richmond: Yes, that's right. That was part of it.

Paul Stillwell: And I guess you said that really, because of the context, you had very little opportunity to evaluate the leadership capabilities. That had presumably been done at an earlier stage.

Mr. Richmond: That's right. I could judge somewhat from meeting them in the classroom. Specifically, they were assigned to shadow these white company commanders, and that was considered part of the leadership training. And we had no untoward incidents that I can remember, other than that one with Martin. It's unfortunate that the chief picked that fellow, because he picked a pretty great guy. He was tampering with something over his head, and he got defeated.

Paul Stillwell: Anything else you recall from that experience that we should put on the record? I think I've about run through my prepared list of questions.

Mr. Richmond: No, Paul, I don't think so. I'd just like to say that it was a very gratifying experience for me, and I thoroughly enjoyed it. I didn't want to have that as my only experience in the Navy—to become an expert on race relations. But it was a pleasant experience for me.

Paul Stillwell: I think one of the measures of how well the Navy picked in selecting these first black officers is that so many of them have been successes in civilian life after leaving the Navy.

Mr. Richmond: Yes, I would say so. It has been the same for blacks and whites as well.

Paul Stillwell: That's certainly true. Anything else for the record?

Mr. Richmond: No, I think that's it, Paul. Shall we wind it up?

Paul Stillwell: I very much appreciate your contribution. It has been a pleasure for me to talk to the black officers themselves, and also a pleasure to see someone who had such an instrumental role in getting them to that place. Thank you.

Mr. Richmond: Thank you, Paul.

Launched in 1969, the U.S. Naval Institute's award-winning oral history program is among the oldest in the country. Used in combination with documentary sources, oral histories offer a richer understanding of naval history through candid recollections and explanations rarely entered into contemporary records. In addition, they help depict the atmosphere of a particular event or era in a manner not available in official documents.

The nonprofit Naval Institute accomplishes its history projects through contributed funds and gratefully accepts tax-deductible gifts of all sizes for this purpose. This support allows the Institute to preserve the life experiences of today's service men and women so they may enlighten and inspire future generations.

For information about opportunities to underwrite Naval Institute oral history projects, please contact the Naval Institute Foundation at 291 Wood Road, Annapolis, Maryland 21402; by phone at (410) 295-1054; or by e-mail at foundation@usni.org.

Index to the Oral History of
Mr. Paul D. Richmond

Antiair Warfare
   Simulator used for antiaircraft gunnery training at Great Lakes, Illinois, in World War II, 18-19

Armstrong, Captain Daniel W., USNR (USNA, 1915)
   Served as officer in charge of Camp Robert Smalls for black sailors at Great Lakes Naval Training Station in World War II, 3-9, 12, 14-17, 21-22

Buhrer, Lieutenant (junior grade) Gordon C., USN (USNA, 1942)
   Served on board the destroyer *Ludlow* (DD-438) during the Allied invasion of North Africa in November 1942, 18-19

Camp Robert Smalls, Great Lakes, Illinois
   Site of recruit training for black sailors in World War II, 3-17
   In 1944 the Navy's first black officers were trained at Great Lakes, 17-33

Chicago, Illinois
   Site of liberty for black sailors undergoing recruit training in World War II, 13

Dille, Lieutenant (junior grade) John F., USNR
   Was involved in training black recruits at the Great Lakes Naval Training Station during World War II, 3-4, 9-11, 14-15, 19, 29, 31

Disciplinary Problems
   Misguided attempt to punish black sailors at the Great Lakes Naval Training Station during World War II, 20-22

Enlisted Personnel
   Recruit training at Great Lakes, Illinois, during World War II, 2-17, 28

Goodwin, Reginald E.
   Member of the Golden Thirteen, the first black naval officers, trained at Great Lakes Naval Training Station in 1944, 14, 30

Great Lakes, Illinois, Naval Training Station
   Training of recruits during World War II, 2-17
   In 1944 the Navy's first black officers were trained at Great Lakes, 17-33
   Near the end of World War II V-7 aviation program dropouts were trained at Great Lakes, 28
   After they were commissioned, the first black officers were not welcome at the base officers' club, 31

Kauffold, Ensign Vance A., USNR
Was involved in training black recruits at the Great Lakes Naval Training Station during World War II, 3-4, 11-12

Lear, Charles B.
Member of the Golden Thirteen, the first black naval officers, trained at Great Lakes Naval Training Station in 1944, 29-30

Leave and Liberty
Liberty in Chicago for black sailors undergoing recruit training in World War II, 13

Louis, Joe
Black boxing champion who was at a club in Chicago during World War II, 13

Martin, Graham E.
Member of the Golden Thirteen, the first black naval officers, trained at Great Lakes Naval Training Station in 1944, 7, 20-24, 30

Nelson, Dennis D. II
Member of the Golden Thirteen, the first black naval officers, trained at Great Lakes Naval Training Station in 1944, 21

Racial Issues
Segregated training for black sailors at Great Lakes Naval Training Station in World War II, 3-16
In 1943 Richmond was discouraged from sending an article to the *Naval Institute Proceedings* on the progress of black sailors in the Navy, 16-17
In 1944 the Navy's first black officers were trained at Great Lakes, 17-29
After they were commissioned, the first black officers were not welcome at the base officers' club, 31

Richmond, Lieutenant Paul D., USNR (USNA, 1942)
Boyhood in the Midwest, 1-2
Naval Academy midshipman, 1938-41, 1-2, 18, 24
Assigned to the Great Lakes Naval Training Station, 1942-44, 1-33

Roosevelt, President Franklin D.
Visited the Great Lakes Naval Training Station in 1944, 5, 16

Shore Patrol
In Chicago for black sailors on liberty in World War II, 13

Training
Recruit training at Great Lakes, Illinois, during World War II, 2-17, 28
In 1944 the Navy's first black officers were trained at Great Lakes, 17-33

Tunney, Lieutenant Commander James J. "Gene," USNR
   In charge of physical training for the Navy during World War II, 9-10

Turek, Commander William, USNR (USNA, 1926)
   During World War II commanded the recruit training organization at the Great Lakes Naval Training Station, 28

Van Ness, Lieutenant (junior grade) Donald O., USNR (USNA, 1935)
   Was involved in training black recruits at the Great Lakes Naval Training Station during World War II, 3-4, 11-12, 17

White, William Sylvester
   Member of the Golden Thirteen, the first black naval officers, trained at Great Lakes Naval Training Station in 1944, 22-23

www.ingramcontent.com/pod-product-compliance
Lightning Source LLC
Chambersburg PA
CBHW082042200426
43209CB00053B/1376